My First Book about the Alphabet of Turtles & Tortoises

I0440486

Amazing Animal Books Children's Picture Books

By Molly Davidson

Mendon Cottage Books

JD-Biz Publishing

Download Free Books!
http://MendonCottageBooks.com

Read More Amazing Animal Books

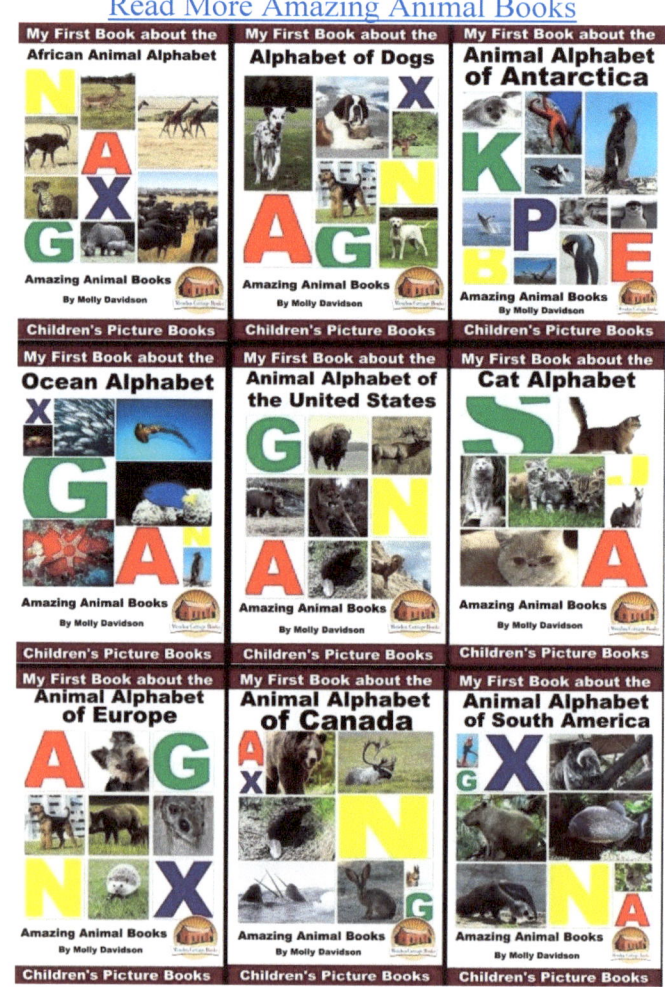

Purchase at Amazon.com

Download Free Books!

http://MendonCottageBooks.com

Introduction

Turtles and tortoises both lay eggs, are cold blooded, and a reptile.

They have lived on the Earth for over 215 million years!

 **is for an Alligator Snapping Turtle.**

An alligator snapping turtle can grow to over 2 1/2 feet long and weigh up to 200 pounds.

They have a very powerful jaw with a hooked beak, which they use to eat fish, frogs, snakes...

B is for a Box Turtle.

During the hot days of summer, box turtles will burrow in the mud under logs or bushes, to help stay cool.

They can survive up to 100 years in the wild, but most live for about 30 years.

C is for a Cagle's Map Turtle.

Mokele © Wikimedia Commons

Cagle's map turtles are only found in three rivers in Texas in the United States.

The boys grow to be only 4 inches long and the girls grow to be about 7 inches long.

They are named at Dr. Cagle, a herpetologist, which is someone who studies amphibians.

D  is for a Diamondback Terrapin.

Diamondback terrapins live in the semi-salt waters from Florida north to Maine in the U.S.

They lay 4 - 22 eggs in sand dunes in the early spring, the babies will hatch by the beginning of the fall.

 **is for an Elongated Tortoise.**

Elongated tortoises are at least twice as long as they are deep, and can grow up to 12 inches long.

They live in Southeast Asia and are an endangered species.

F is for a Flatback Sea Turtle.

Purpleturtle57 © Wikimedia Commons

Flatback sea turtles only live in the coastal waters of Australia and Papua New Guinea.

They lay about 50 eggs on sandy beaches, four times per year.

Adults can grow to weigh up to 200 pounds and 3 1/4 feet long.

G is for a Green Sea Turtle.

Green sea turtles are one of the largest sea turtles, weighing up to 420 pounds.

They are found in all the tropical oceans throughout the World.

They are named after the green fat found under their shells.

G is also for a Galapagos Tortoise.

Galapagos tortoises are the largest living tortoises, weighing up to 900 pounds!

They live for over 100 years in the wild and over 170 years in zoos.

 is for a Hermann's Tortoise.

Hermann's tortoises are found throughout southern Europe.

They sleep in hollows during the night and come out during the day to soak up the sun, in order to get warm.

I is for an Indian Star Tortoise.

The Indian star tortoise lives in the dry forests of Sri Lanka and India.

Their unique star patterned shell helps them blend in with their environment making it harder for predators to see them.

J is for a Jamaican Slider.

Charlesjsharp © Wikimedia Commons

Jamaican sliders are also called cat island sliders, and are found in the freshwaters of the Bahamas and Jamaica.

They eat lots of fruit, small fish, snails, and frogs.

 **is for a Kemp's Ridley Sea Turtle.**

Kemp's ridley sea turtles have strong jaws
which they use to crush clams, crabs, mussels,
shrimp, jellyfish, and sea urchins.

Adults are a dark grey green color and the
babies (called hatchlings) are black.

L is for a Leatherback Sea Turtle.

Leatherback turtles are the largest of all turtles, and can weigh up to 2,000 pounds.

They are the only sea turtle to have a soft shell, which is made of thin, tough, rubbery skin, made strong by thousands of tiny bone plates.

 **is for a Mud Turtle.**

Mud turtles are also called kinosternon, and are found all over the United States, Mexico, and South America.

They eat fish, insects, and sometimes flesh of dead animals.

Raccoons love to eat their eggs, and alligators and herons like to eat adult mud turtles.

M is also for a Matamata Turtle.

© Wikimedia Commons

Matamata turtles live the Amazon and Orinoco river basins in South America.

Their spiky shell looks like tree bark, and their heads look like leaves, this is how they blend in with their environment.

 **is for a Nile Softshell Turtle.**

Nile softshell turtles are found throughout Africa in fresh water.

They live an average of 50 years in the wild.

They have a long triangular nose with nostrils on the end; this is different than most turtles.

O

is for an Olive Ridley Sea Turtle.

Olive ridley sea turtles lay their eggs in a nest made in the coastal sandy beaches, here they lay around 110 eggs, two times per year.

The babies are a grey color, and the adults are an olive green color (this is where they get their name from).

P is for a Painted Turtle.

Painted turtles live in ponds from southern Canada all the way south to Mexico.

Mother turtles dig nests in the sand close to water to lay their 5 - 12 eggs.

Fossils have been found of painted turtles which are 15 million years old.

P is also for a Pancake Tortoise.

Pancake tortoises have a flat shell, that's where their name comes from.

They live in Tanzania and Kenya, on the dry savannahs.

The babies are able to take care of themselves as soon as they hatch.

 **is for a Roofed Turtle.**

Nandini Velho © <u>Wikimedia Commons</u>

Roofed turtles are very common in South Asia, and are kept by many as pets.

They live in ponds and eat the vegetation and snails growing there.

They like to lie in the morning sun to get warm and get their daily dose of Vitamin D.

R is also for a Red-Eared Terrapin.

Red -eared terrapin are found all over the United States and are the most common turtle kept as a pet all over the World.

The comic books, <u>Teenage Mutant Ninja Turtles</u>, were designed after the red-eared terrapin.

S is for a Side-Necked Turtle.

Johannes van Rooyen © <u>Wikimedia Commons</u>

Side-necked turtles get their name from the way they tuck their head into their shell sideways, instead of straight back.

They live in South America, Australia, New Guinea, and Indonesia.

T is for a Texas Tortoise.

Clinton & Charles Robertson © <u>Wikimedia Commons</u>

Texas tortoises grow to have a shell that is 8 1/2 inches long.

They do not start to lay eggs until they are 15 years old, but they live to be about 60 years old, in the wild.

 **is for a Western Pond Turtle.**

Yathin S Krishnappa © <u>Wikimedia Commons</u>

Western pond turtles are only found in fresh water lakes and ponds, on the west coast of the United States, from Washington state south to Baja, California.

W

is also for a Wood Turtle.

Wood turtles travel fast on land, for a turtle, about 1/4 of a mile per hour.

As they get older the boys become more aggressive, and the larger ones have the most control.

 **is for a Yellow-Footed Tortoise.**

Yellow-footed tortoises are also called Brazilian giant tortoises, because their shells grow to be 16 inches long.

The boys will swing their heads back and forth as a way to communicate with each other.

Conclusion

I hope you have enjoyed reading about some amazing turtles.

One last fact, the main difference between a turtle and a tortoise is turtles live mostly in water and tortoises live on land.

Read More Animal Alphabet Books!!

Download Free Books!

http://MendonCottageBooks.com

Purchase at Amazon.com
Website http://AmazingAnimalBooks.com

Our books are available at

1. Amazon.com

2. Barnes and Noble

3. Itunes

4. Kobo

5. Smashwords

6. Google Play Books

Download Free Books!
http://MendonCottageBooks.com

Publisher

JD-Biz Corp

P O Box 374

Mendon, Utah 84325

http://www.jd-biz.com/

www.ingramcontent.com/pod-product-compliance
Lightning Source LLC
Chambersburg PA
CBHW050857290526
45792CB00002B/628